Compiled by The Editors at T~~~~~~~ ~~~~~
Illustrated by Sarah Perez

an imprint of
~~ ~~~~~~~ ~~~~~
www.scholastic.com

Copyright 2004 Scholastic Inc.

Scholastic and Tangerine Press and associated logos are trademarks of Scholastic Inc.
Published by Tangerine Press, an imprint of Scholastic Inc; 557 Broadway, New York, NY 10012

10 9 8 7 6 5 4 3 2 1

ISBN: 0-439-68984-8

Printed and bound in Canada

# Warning:

Humor may be hazardous to your bad mood!

# Laugh Out Loud

**What do you get when
an elephant skydives?**
A big hole.

**Why is that
skyscraper sneezing?**
It has a building code.

**How do you get six elephants
in a matchbox?**
First, take out the matches.

## How do you milk an ant?

First you get a very low stool...

## How does an elephant get out of a small car?

The same way he got in.

**Which chicken is the meanest?**
Attila the Hen.

**How does the man on the moon hold up his pants?**
With an asteroid belt.

**What is brown and sticky?**
A stick.

**How do you catch a runaway computer?**
With an Internet.

**How do you fix a tomato?**
Use tomato paste.

**How do you make a car smile?**
Take it on a joy ride.

**Where do snowmen put their money?**
In a snowbank.

**Did you ever see a sidewalk?**
No, but I've seen a nose run.

**Did you ever hear the rope joke?**
Skip it.

**Why did the music students get in trouble?**
They were passing notes.

**Why did the trumpet player go to the dentist?**
He needed a toot canal.

**Why was the broom late for school?**
It overswept.

**Who was Snow White's brother?**
Egg white. Get the yoke?

**How do you make a clock laugh?**
Tick, tick, tick-lish.

**Someday I want to be cloned.**
Why make a fool of yourself.

**I have a splinter in my finger.**
Scratching your head again?

**Who can jump higher than a house?**
Anyone, houses can't jump.

**Why is twice ten the same as twice eleven?**
Because twice ten is twenty, and twice eleven is twenty, too.

**Why do you keep a trumpet in the fridge?**
So it plays cool music.

**Why does Santa climb down the chimney?**

It soots him.

**Is it dangerous to swim on a full stomach?**

It's better to swim in water.

**Why did the golfer wear an extra pair of pants?**

In case he got a hole in one.

**What is Santa's favorite cowboy song?**
HO-HO Home on the Range.

**What state is always happy?**
Merryland.

**Did you hear about the Broadway musical with sardines?**
They are really packing them in.

**How do you fix a cracked pumpkin?**
With a
pumpkin patch.

**What should
you do if
you swallow
a spoon?**
Lie down and
don't stir.

**Why did the woman spray her computer with insect repellent?**
A program had a bug in it.

**Why would you bring scissors to dinner?**
To cut calories.

**What do teenage geese worry about?**
Getting goose pimples.

**What happened at the milking competition?**

Udder chaos.

**How do vegetables trace their family tree?**

They go back to their roots.

**What do computer programmers eat for a snack?**

Chips.

**What is made of wood,
but can't be sawed?**
Sawdust.

**What happened when
the wheel was invented?**
It caused a revolution.

**What's bent, salty,
and sings?**
Elvis Pretzel.

What has 12 tails, 6 eyes,
3 tails, and can't see?
Three blind mice.

What state can
tell the most jokes?
Jokelahoma.

How does Jack Frost
get around?
By icicle.

How do you know where
an escaped train is hiding?
Just follow the tracks.

What did the artist say when
he had to choose a pencil?
2B or not 2B, that
is the question.

What animal lives
on your head?
A hare.

**What do you give a sick snake?**
Asp-rin.

**What do you get from
an angry sewing machine?**
Cross stitches.

**Where does Tarzan
the vampire bite people?**
In the Jungular.

**How do you get rid of a boomerang?**
Throw it down a
one way street.

**How do you find a lost dog?**
Put your ear to a tree and listen
for the bark.

**How did the computer hacker get out of jail?**
He pressed the escape key.

# Where can you find a lot of shoes?
In the foothills.

**Why do you go to bed?**
Because the bed won't
come to you.

**What is the best
way to stuff a turkey?**
Take him out for a nice dinner.

**What word can a dog actually say?**
BARK!

**What do porcupines say when they kiss?**
Ouch.

**Why are tomatoes a slow fruit?**
They are always trying to catch up.

**What do Eskimos eat for breakfast?**
Ice Krispies.

**What's the hardest thing about riding a horse?**
The ground.

**Where would you find a flexible trumpet?**
In a rubber band.

**What boats do smart kids travel on?**
Scholar-ships.

**Why was the computer angry?**
It had a chip on its shoulder.

**Have you heard the joke
about the peach?**
It's pitiful.

**What is hairy and writes?**
A ballpoint bunny.

# Game Time

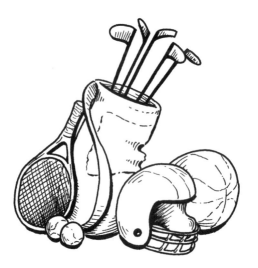

What stories do basketball
players read?
**Tall tales.**


What is a runner's favorite
school subject?
**Jog-raphy.**


What lights up a
football stadium?
**A football game.**

What do you call a 100 year old cheerleader?
**Old Yeller**

What do you get if you cross a baker and a prizefighter?
**A bread boxer.**

What's a sailor's favorite magazine?
**Ports Illustrated.**

What would you get if you crossed a newborn snake with a basketball?
**A bouncing baby boa.**

What does a coach do for chickens at halftime?
**He gives them a peep talk.**

Is the locksmith a good baseball player?
**He's a key player.**

What's red, green, and wears
boxing gloves?
**Fruit punch.**

What's the difference
between a nail and a boxer?
**One gets knocked in and the
other gets knocked out.**

What does a boxer drink?
**Punch.**

What do you think of the new jogging suit?
**I don't know. Run it by me again.**

What is the difference between an exhausted runner and a burned-out vet?
**One is dog-tired, and the other is tired of dogs.**

Why was the baseball player
arrested in the middle
of the game?
**He was stealing second base.**

Why is a tent like baseball?
**They both have to be pitched.**

Why are baseball players
so cool?
**They have so many fans.**

Why did the coach send in the second string?
**To tie up the game.**

What job does Dracula have with the Transylvanian baseball team?
**Bat-boy.**

What is the noisiest sport?
**Tennis–What a racket!**

Why don't you go outside and play football with your little brother?
**I'd rather play with a regular football.**

Why is a bad golfer like a motorboat?
**They both go putt, putt, putt, putt...**

Did you hear about the
Siamese twin golfers?
**They had a tee for two.**

Where does a train exercise?
**On a train track.**

What do you call basketball
nets in Hawaii?
**Hula Hoops.**

Which TV sports program
is less filling?
**Monday Lite Football.**

How are a baseball game and
pancakes similar?
**They both depend on the
batter.**

Where do ferris wheels
go in October?
**The whirl series.**

When is fishing not healthy
for you?
**When you are a worm.**

Which baseball team does
George Stybrenner own?
**The New Pork Yankees.**

Why do basketball players stay
home during the season?
**They aren't allowed to travel.**

What do you call a person
that tells bad jokes while
she's running?
**A cross country punner.**

Why did the quarterback yell
hut, hut, ah-choo?
**It's football sneezin'.**

Did you hear about the football game with a 0-0 score?
**It was pointless.**

Why did the boys go to basketball camp?
**They wanted to grow by leaps and rebounds.**

What do you get if your receivers don't lift weights at practice?
**Weak ends.**

When does a skier stop going downhill?
**When she reaches the bottom.**

What bet can never be won?
**The Alphabet.**

Why did Cinderella get thrown off the baseball team?
**She ran away from the ball.**

What's the difference between a baby and a basketball player?
**One drools and the other dribbles.**

Why was Cinderella such
a bad player?
**Her coach was a pumpkin.**

What has 18 legs and
catches flies?
**A baseball team.**

Why did the soccer ball
quit the team?
**It was tired of being
kicked around.**

Why did the volleyball go
to the bank?
**It wanted to find its net
worth.**

Why can't you play sports
in the jungle?
**Because of all the cheetahs.**

What should you do when 19
guys are running at you?
**Throw the football.**

Why does it take longer to run from second base to third base than it takes to run from first to second?
**There is a short stop between second and third.**

Which baseball team also takes care of sick animals?
**The New York Vets.**

What kind of football player has the biggest helmet?
**The one with the biggest head.**

Why didn't the nose make the volleyball team?
**He didn't get picked.**

What is the biggest diamond in the world?
**A baseball diamond.**

Did you hear about the
marathon runner who
worked as a chimney sweep?
**He was a great runner, but
suffered from athlete's soot.**

What is the difference
between a boxer and
a man with a cold?
**One knows his blows and
the other blows his nose.**

How did the basketball
court get wet?
**The players dribbled all over
it.**

Why didn't the dog play
baseball?
**It was a boxer.**

How do you stop squirrels from
playing baseball?
**Take away the ball.
It drives them nuts.**

Why do artist's never win
when playing basketball?
**They always draw the foul.**

What are Brazilian
soccer fans called?
**Brazil nuts.**

What are the seasons
for a sports fan?
**Basketball, baseball,
hockey, and football.**

Why shouldn't you tell jokes
while ice skating?
**The ice might crack up.**

What do quarterbacks
like to eat?
**Hut, hut, hut dogs.**

Where do old bowling
balls end up?
**In the gutter.**

# Is it better to be a Jock or a Nerd?

- Michael Jordan made over $300,000 per game. That's $10,000 a minute, if he plays 30 minutes per game.
- If you were given a tenth of a penny for every dollar he made, you'd be living on $65,000 a year.

## Amazing right?

- But, Michael Jordan will have to save 100 percent of his income for 270 years to have a net worth equivalent to that of Bill Gates.

Bobby swung the door open after his Little League game. His Mother asked, "So, how did you do?"

"You'll never believe it!" Billy said. "I was responsible for the winning run!"

"Really? How'd you do that?" asked his Mother.

"I dropped the ball."

# Top Ten New Rules for Little League Baseball:

1. Catch a foul ball, win the allowance of the guy who hit it.
2. Infield chatter must be in the form of a question.
3. No more keeping your eye on the ball.
4. All players must squat like a catcher for the entire game.
5. Instead of the National Anthem, sing (insert favorite song here).

## Skier's Dictionary:

**Alp:** A shout for assistance when you're buried in snow.

**Bones:** There are 206 in the human body. The bones in the middle ear have never been broken while skiing.

**Shin:** The bruised area on the front of the leg that runs from the wrenched knee to the sprained ankle.

**Skier:** One who pays an arm and a leg for the opportunity to break them.

**Traverse:** To ski across the slope at an angle to reduce your speed.

**Tree:** The other method of reducing your speed.

Soccer players are great in school because they use their heads.

What has 22 legs and goes, "Crunch, crunch, crunch?"
**A soccer team eating potato chips.**

What race is never run?
**A swimming race.**

**Murphy's Sports Law:** Exciting plays only happen when you're watching the scoreboard or buying a hot dog.

# Animal Farm

# Why did the bear go over the mountain?

He couldn't go under it.

# How did the kangaroo get into the school?

He came through the door.

# What do cats like to drink?

Mice tea.

**What is black, white, brown, and red all over?**
A Chihuahua in a tuxedo that tripped into a jar of salsa.

**What do you call a talkative monkey?**
A blaboon.

**When is it unlucky to see a black cat?**
When you're a mouse.

**What is the difference between a camel and a strawberry?**
A strawberry is red.

**How do you stop a mouse from squeaking?**
Oil it.

**How does a leopard keep his house?**
Spotless.

**What do you call a lion wearing headphones?**

Anything you want.
He can't hear you.


**What is big, gray, and puts quarters under the pillows of baby elephants?**

The tusk fairy.

**What is a skunk's favorite children's book?**
Winnie the P-U!

**What is the world's strongest animal?**
A snail. It carries its house on its back.

**What do snakes write on the bottom of their letters?**
With love and hisses.

**Where do cool mice live?**
In mouse pads.

**Where do whales
look up definitions?**
In a Moby Dicktionary.

**What kind of fish do
you eat with peanut butter?**
Jellyfish.

**What do frogs like to drink on cold days?**
Hot croako.

**Did you hear about the man who crossed a centipede with a turkey?**
For Thanksgiving, everyone got a drumstick.

**What has an elephant's trunk, a tiger's stripes, a giraffe's neck, and a baboon's funny nose?**

A zoo.

**Why was the kangaroo mother mad at her children?**

They were jumping on the bed.

**What is a reptile's favorite movie?**

The Lizard of Oz.

**What is big, white, and furry, and found in Australia?**
A very lost polar bear.

**Where do bees go when they're sick?**
The waspital.

**What do you call a deer with only one eye?**
No Idea.

**What animal drops from the sky?**
Rain deer.

**What is big, gray, and wears a glass slipper?**
Cinderelephant.

**What goes "99 bonk"?**
A centipede with a wooden leg.

**What did one flea say to the other?**
Shall we hop or take the dog?

**Where do cows go for fun?**
Mooovies.

**What is a cats favorite treat?**
Mice Cream.

**What kind of shoes do frogs where in the summer?**
Open Toad Sandals.

**What do you call an unmarried female moth?**
Myth.

**What did the 100 pound parrot say?**
"Polly want a cracker, NOW!"

**What does a vulture always have for dinner?**
Leftovers.

**What does an educated owl say?**
"Whom."

**Why is an owl smarter than a chicken?**
You've never heard of a "Kentucky Fried Owl" have you?

**What do you call an elephant in a telephone booth?**
Stuck.

**What is the difference between a bird and fly?**
A bird can fly, but a fly can't bird.

**What's the difference between a guitar and a fish?**
You can tune a guitar, but you can't tuna fish.

**Why do birds fly south?**
It's too far to walk.

**What kind of bees fight?**
Rumble bees.

**What kind of sharks don't eat women?**
Man-eating sharks.

What does a crab use
to make a phone call?
A shell phone.

Why did the fish cross the ocean?
To get to the other tide.

What do you call a
fish with no eyes?
Fsh.

# Why was the elephant standing on the marshmallow?

He didn't want to fall in the hot chocolate.

What do you get if you cross
a centipede with a parrot?
A walkie-talkie.

Why did the crow sit
on the telephone line?
To make a long distance caw.

Why did the spider use
the computer?
It was looking for
a new website.

**What did the dog say when he was attacked by a tiger?**
Nothing, dogs can't talk.

**What do you get from a nervous cow?**
A milk shake.

**What do you call a frog with no legs?**
Unhoppy.

# Knock, Knock

**Knock, Knock**

Who's there?

**Ben!**

Ben Who?

**Ben knocking all day.**


**Knock, Knock**

Who's there?

**Armageddon**

Armageddon who?

**Armageddon outta here.**

**Knock, Knock**
Who's there?
**A Fred.**
A Fred who?
**I was a fred you wouldn't
open the door.**


**Knock, knock**
Who's there?
**Rocky**
Rocky who?
**Rocky bye baby on the tree tops!**

**Knock, Knock**
Who's there?
**Diss**
Diss who?
**Diss is a dumb knock,
knock joke.**

**Knock, knock**
Who's there?
**Oppa.**
Oppa who?
**Oppa-tunity knocking!**

**Knock, Knock**

Who's there?

**Dozen**

Dozen who?

**Dozen anyone know who I am?**


**Knock, knock**

Who's there?

**Ogre.**

Ogre who?

**Ogre the hill and far away!**

**Knock, Knock**

Who's there?

**Lass**

Lass who?

**Go get ém cowboy.**

**Knock, knock**

Who's there?

**Lena.**

Lena who?

**Lena a little closer I have a secret.**

**Knock, knock**
Who's there?
**Ooze.**
Ooze who?
**Ooze in charge around here!**

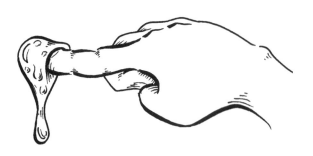

**Knock, Knock**

Who's there?

**Noah.**

Noah who?

**Noah good place to eat?**


**Knock, knock**

Who's there?

**Nobody!**

Nobody who?

**Just nobody!**

**Knock, Knock**
Who's there?
**Pecan**
Pecan who?
**Pecan someone your own size.**

**Knock, knock**
Who's there?
**Midas**
Midas who?
**Midas well let me in!**

**Knock, Knock.**
Who's there?
**Sancho.**
Sancho who?
**Sancho a letter yesterday.**

**Knock, knock**
Who's there?
**Lettuce.**
Lettuce who?
**Lettuce in it's cold out here!**

**Knock, Knock**

Who's there?

**Little old lady.**

Little old lady who?

**I didn't know you could yodel.**

**Knock, knock**

Who's there?

**Juno!**

Juno who?

**I know who, do you know who?**

**Knock, Knock**

Who's there?

**Fido.**

Fido who?

**Fido known you were coming I would've cleaned up.**

**Knock, knock**

Who's there?

**Havana.**

Havana who?

**Havana a great time!**

**Knock, knock**
Who's there?
**Chicken!**
Chicken who?
**Chicken your pocket for the keys.**

Knock, knock
Who's there?
Carrie
Carrie who?
Carrie me. I'm tired.

Knock, knock
Who's there?
Amiss!
Amiss who?
Amiss you! That's why I'm here!

Knock, knock
Who's there?
Costas.
Costas who?
Costas a lot to get here.

Knock, knock
Who's there?
Anna
Anna who?
Annather knock, knock joke!

**Knock, knock**

Who's there?

**Cologne.**

Cologne who?

**Cologne me names is not nice.**


**Knock, knock**

Who's there?

**Europe**

Europe who?

**Europe bright and early!**

Knock, knock
Who's there?
Crete.
Crete who?
Crete to meet you.


Knock, knock
Who's there?
Wade
Wade who?
Wade a minute, I'll get my key!

**Knock, knock**
Who's there?
**C-2**
C-2 who?
**C-2 it that your room is clean.**

**Knock, knock**
Who's there?
**You.**
You who?
**Hello!**

Knock, knock
Who's there?
Giraffe.
Giraffe who?
Giraffe to ask me that question

Knock, knock
Who's there?
Mike
Mike who?
Mike up your mind!

Knock, knock
Who's there?
Belle.
Belle who?
Belle don't work, so knock.


Knock, knock
Who's there?
Ginger
Ginger who?
Ginger hear the doorbell?

**Knock, knock**
Who's there?
**Denise.**
Denise who?
**Denise are knockin' cause I'm scared.**

**Knock, knock**
Who's there?
**Kent**
Kent who?
**Kent you stop asking questions
and open the door!**

**Knock, knock**
Who's there?
**Yul.**
Yul who?
**Yul see when you open the door.**

**Knock, knock**
Who's there?
**Trish**
Trish who?
**Bless you!**

**Knock, knock**
Who's there?
Colin.
Colin who?
**Colin to see if you want to go to the movies.**

**Knock, knock**
Who's there?
**Jester.**
Jester who?
**Jester day, all my troubles
seemed so far away.**


**Knock, knock**
Who's there?
**Wendy**
Wendy who?
**Wendy you want me to come by?**

**Knock, knock**
Who's there?
**Seymour**
Seymour who?
**Seymour of me when you
open the door.**


**Knock, knock**
Who's there?
**Will**
Will who?
**Will I have to wait long?**

**Knock, knock**
Who's there?
**Ken.**
Ken who?
**Ken you come out and play?**

**Knock, knock**
Who's there?
**Woody**
Woody who?
**Woody open the door if
we asked him nicely?**

Knock, knock
Who's there?
**Guess Simon.**
Guess Simon who?
**Guess Simon knockin' on
the wrong door.**

**Knock, knock**
Who's there?
**Penny.**
Penny who?
**Penny for your thoughts.**

**Knock, knock**
Who's there?
**Frank**
Frank who?
**Frank you for opening the door!**

# Gross Giggles

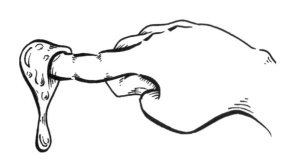

What is hairy and coughs?
**A coconut with a cold.**

Why did the skull go to
the dance by himself?
**He had no body
to go with.**

What kind of ghost would
you find up your nose?
**A Boogerman!**

How can you tell if
a moth farts?
**He flies straight
for a second.**

How do you keep flies
out of the kitchen?
**Take out the garbage.**

What does a cannibal
doctor charge?
**An arm and a leg.**

What do you call pigs that
write to each other?
**Pen pals.**

What is the only thing you
can lose but still have?
**Your temper.**

What is a volcano?
**A headless mountain.**

What has 50 feet,
but can't walk?
**A tape measure.**

What has 100 feet but can't
walk, and it's not a tape
measure?
**A dead centipede.**

What driver has never
passed a driving test?
**A screw driver.**

Why did the fool drive
his car off the mountain?
**Someone told him it
had air brakes.**

What does a frog do
when it dies?
**It croaks.**

Why did the cannibal
have indigestion?
**He must have
eaten someone that
disagreed with him.**

What does a skeleton
like to eat?
**Ribs.**

Which two letters are bad for
your teeth?
**D. K.**

What did the mother sardine
say to her baby when they saw
a submarine?
**Don't worry. It's just a
can of people.**

What's a cannibal's
favorite game?
**Swallow the leader.**

What do sea
monsters eat?
**Fish and ships.**

What do you call Mom
and Dad ghosts?
**Transparents**

What do you call a skeleton detective?
**Sherlock bones.**

What is Dr. Jekyll's favorite game?
**Hyde and Seek.**

I have 5 noses, 6 ears, 4 mouths. What am I?
**UGLY!**

What did one toilet say
to the other?
**You look flushed.**

What's the difference
between school lunches
and a pile of slugs?
**School lunches are
on plates.**

Why did the cannibal
eat the tourist?
**He wanted take out.**

Why did the toilet
paper roll down hill?
**To get to the bottom.**

Why did the surfer
stop surfing?
**The sea weed.**

What is the soft stuff
between a sharks teeth?
**Slow swimmers.**

Why did Dracula take
some medicine?
**To stop his coffin.**

What do you find in
a clean nose?
**Fingerprints.**

What did the cannibal say
when he was full?
**I couldn't eat
another mortal.**

What's invisible and smells
like carrots?
**Bunny farts.**

Why do gorillas have
big nostrils?
**They have big fingers.**

What do you give an
elephant with diarrhea?
**A lot of room.**

Did you hear the
fart joke?
**It stinks.**

What has 50 feet,
but can't walk?
**Half a centipede.**

What is green and red
and goes 125 mph?
**A frog in a blender.**

What's yellow and smells
like bananas?
**Monkey vomit.**

How do you make
a tissue dance?
**Put some boogie into it.**

What do you do if your nose
goes on strike?
**Picket.**

What do you give
a sick elephant?
**A very big
paperbag.**

What's the difference
between a maggot and
a cockroach?
**Cockroaches crunch when
you eat them.**

What's the last thing that
goes through a bug's mind
when it hits the windshield?
**His backside.**

# What do you call...

What do you call a man
with very thick glasses?
**Seymour.**

What do you call a little woman
who laughs alot?
**Minnie ha ha.**

What do you call a woman with
a frog on her head?
**Lily.**

What do you call a girl
who sells parrots?
**Polly.**

What do you call a
frightened man?
**Hugo first.**

What do you call a
failed lion tamer?
**Claude Bottom.**

What do you call a man
that doesn't sink?
**Bob.**

What do you call the super
heroes that got run over?
**Flatman and Ribbon.**

What do you call a man with
a computer on his head?
**Mac.**

What do you call a sick
martial arts expert?
**Kung Flu.**

What do you call a woman
who works at the zoo?
**Ellie Fant.**

What do you call a man
with a male alleycat?
**Tom.**

What do you call a girl
that gets up early?
**Dawn.**

What do you call a man with
a lot of money?
**Bill.**

What do you call a woman
with a ball of wool?
**Barbara Black Sheep.**

What do you call a
woman on a sinking ship?
**Mandy Lifeboats.**

What do you call
a girl with
a head made
of glass?
**Crystal.**

What do you call a man that deals
with legal documents?
**Will.**

What do you call a man driving
on the sidewalk?
**Ron Way.**

What do you call a man
with an anvil?
**Smith.**

What do you call a woman with
her hand in the butter?
**Marge.**

What do you call a
girl at the beach?
**Sandy.**

What do you call a ghost that
haunts a TV talk show?
**Phantom of the Oprah.**

What do you call a man
with a roadmap?
**Miles.**

What do you call a woman with a
large, fiery, ball of gas on her head?
**Sunny.**

What do you call a girl
with half a lizard?
**Liz.**

What do you call a man with a bear?
Teddy.

What do you call a man with some stinky cheese?
Gordon Zola.

What do you call a vampire with a calculator?
The Count.

What do you call
an overweight vampire?
**Draculard.**

What do you call a man
that sings karoake?
**Mike.**

What do you call a boy that does
everything to the extreme?
**Max.**

What do you call a man that fishes
a lot?
**Rod.**

What do you call a man that likes
drawing and painting?
**Art.**

What do you call a man that keeps
an angry ferret in his pants?
**Not too smart.**

What do you call a 350 pound
sumo wrestler?
**Whatever he wants you to.**

What do you call a woman who
crosses a river?
**Bridget.**

What do you call a man that waits
by your front door all day?
**Matt.**

What do you call a boy
with a goat?
**Billy.**

What do you call a girl with
a lot of suitcases?
**Carrie.**

What do you call a teacher
who has a lot of accidents?
**Miss Hap.**

What do you call a cat
that eats lemons?
**Sour Puss.**

What do you call a jogger in a safari park?
**Fast food.**

What do you call the pudding that fought at Little Big Horn?
**General Custard.**

What do you call a tiny version of one of the Beatles?
**Small McCartney.**

What do you call a very
young bee?
**A Ba-Bee.**

What do you call a bee
with its own car?
**A Bee-M-W.**

What do you call a
Russian gardener?
**Ivanhoe.**

What do you call a woman that fell
off a cliff?
**Eileen Dover.**

What do you call a dead parrot?
**Polygon.**

What do you call an animal that
eats weeds?
**Dan de Lion.**

What do you call a ghost's horse?
**A nightmare.**

What do you call a woman that
sneezes all the time, and likes
knock, knock jokes?
**Tish who.**

What do you call a lady
with a crown?
**Your Majesty.**

# Rib-Ticklers

I have ten legs, twenty arms,
and fifty-four feet.
What am I?
**A liar.**


What did the pencil
sharpener say to the pencil?
**Stop going around in circles
and get to the point.**

What do Alexander the Great and Kermit the Frog have in common?
**The same middle name.**


There are three kinds of people in the world. Those who can count. And those who can't.

What's easy to get into but
hard to get out of?
**Trouble.**

What has many rings,
but no fingers?
**A telephone.**

What happens if you
jump into the red sea?
**You get wet.**

What do you call a
lazy toy?
**An inaction figure.**

What do all the Smiths in the
phonebook have in common?
**They all have phones.**

What did one raindrop
say to the others?
**Two's company,
three's a cloud.**

Why did the traffic
light turn red?
**You would too if you had
to change in the middle
of a busy intersection.**

What did the Pacific Ocean
say to the Atlantic Ocean?
**Nothing. It just waved.**

What kind of star is dangerous?
**A shooting star.**

What's the difference between an elephant and a matterbaby?
**What's a matterbaby?**
Nothing, but thanks for asking.

What did the clock's big hand
say to the little hand?
**Got a minute?**

When does B come after U?
**When you've taken some
of its honey.**

Where are the Andes?
**At the end of your armies.**

Did I tell you about the really high brick wall? **I better not. You might not get over it.**

What would you call Superman if he lost all his powers? **Man.**

What has 100 legs,
but can't walk?
**Fifty pairs of pants.**

What birds are found
in Portugal?
**Portu-geese**

Name three famous poles.
**North, South, and tad.**

What jam can't you eat?
**A traffic jam.**

What do you get
if you cross a
dinosaur with
a termite?
**A huge bug
that eats
big buildings
for breakfast.**

How do fishermen
make nets?
**They make a lot of holes
and tie them together
with string.**

What's the difference
between a bus driver
and a cold?
**One knows the stops, the
other stops the nose.**

How did the octopus
couple walk down
the road?
**Arm in arm, in arm,
in arm, in arm, in arm,
in arm, in arm...**

Name six things smaller
than an ant's mouth.
**Six of its teeth.**

What does every
winner lose in a race?
**His breath.**

What goes up, but does
not come down?
**Your age.**

What is the only
cure for dandruff?
**Baldness.**

What gets bigger and bigger the more you take away from it?
**A hole.**

What question can you never answer "yes" to?
**Are you asleep?**

What goes through water, but doesn't get wet?
**A ray of light.**

What belongs to you,
but is used the most
by other people?
**Your name.**

What can you hold
without touching?
**Your breath.**

What is big, red,
and eats rocks?
**A big, red rockeater.**

Why do firemen wear
red suspenders?
**To keep their pants up.**

How many apples can
you put in an empty box?
**One, after that
it's not empty.**

What's red, and goes
up and down?
**A tomato on an elevator.**

What is always coming
but never arrives?
**Tomorrow.**

What kind of dress can
never be worn?
**An address.**

What word is always
spelled incorrectly?
**Incorrectly.**

What can you serve
but never eat?
**A tennis ball.**

When is it bad luck to be followed by a big, black cat? **When you're a little, gray mouse.**

What do you call a musical insect? **A humbug.**

What is the best thing to take into the desert? **A thirst-aid kit.**

Who do you call two
identically masked men?
**The clone rangers.**

What kind of tree
is found in the
kitchen?
**A pantry.**

What lives under the sea
and carries a lot of people?
**An octobus.**


How do you prevent water
from getting into your house?
**Stop paying the water bill.**

What can fill a whole house,
but still weigh less than
a mouse?
**Smoke.**

What do you get if
you cross an acrobat
with a novel?
**A book that can flip
its own pages.**

Why is an empty wallet
always the same?
**Because there's no
change in it.**


What kind of music
does MTV play on
St. Patrick's Day?
**Shamrock & Roll.**

What do you call two
bees, a hornet, and
a wasp with violins?
**A sting quartet.**

What goes best with
an oyster cracker?
**Pearl Jam.**

What do you get if you
cross a dinosaur and a pig?
**Jurassic Pork.**

How many spoiled brats does it take to change a lightbulb?

**Just one. He holds it in the socket and waits for the world to revolve around him.**

What do you get if you cross a cocker spaniel, a poodle, and a rooster?

**A cockerpoodledoo.**

Who has black feathers and
anchors the nightly news?
**Tom Brocaw.**

What's totally silly and
makes dogs itch?
**The Flea Stooges.**

Who styles Bugs Bunny's fur?
**A Hollywood Haredresser.**

What do you get when
you cross Chris Rock
and a lizard?
**A stand-up chameleon.**

What did Cinderella wear
to the undersea ball?
**A glass flipper.**

What's blue and used
to ride waves?
**A smurfboard.**

What is the name of
the millionaire elephant
who owns a hotel
and casino?
**Donald Trunk.**

Who's chocolatey and
drew Mickey Mouse?
**Malt Disney.**

Where do fish sleep?
**In a waterbed.**

What kind of music
was invented by fish?
**Sole music.**

What happened after the
wheel was invented?
**It caused a revolution.**

How do archaeologists
get into locked tombs?
**They use a skeleton key.**

# Dumb Dictionary

**Actor** - a person who works really hard at not being himself.

**Infantry** - a day-care center.

**Khakis** - a necessity for a car to start.

**Zinc** - what you do if you can't zwim.

**Secret** - what we tell everyone not to tell anyone.

**Paralyze** - a couple of fibs.

**Gossip** - person with a great sense of rumor.

**Grudge** - a place to keep your car.

**Bacteria** - the backdoor of the cafeteria.

**Diploma** - the person you call when your sink backs up.

**Calculator** - a product you can count on.

**Diet Plan** - fast thinking.

**Fortification** - two twentifica-
tions.

**Kleptomania** - the gift of grab.

**Bathmats** - small dry rugs that
children stand next to.

**Seamstress** - a real material girl.

**Microwave** - a head full of tiny curls.

**Dog Obedience school** - a make-rover class.

**Skeletons** - a stack of bones with the people scraped off.

**Rollerblading** - a new fall sport.

**Dr. Frankenstein** - a champion body builder.

**Cashew** - the noise a nut makes when it sneezes.

**Swing set** - a place where you hope push comes to shove.

**Flypaper** - what kites are made of.

**Little Miss Muffet** - a lady who knows how to make her whey in the world.

**Bore** - a person who talks about himself, when you'd much rather talk about yourself.

**Paradox** - a couple of physicians.

**Dieting** - the punishment for exceeding the feed limit.

**Digital computer** - someone who counts on his fingers.

**Parapets** - a dog and a cat.

**Artery** - a artist's studio.

**Fireflies** - mosquitos with flash-lights.

**Europe** - what the umpire says when it's your turn at bat.

**Tumor** - an extra pair.

**Cauterize** - got her attention.

**Graffiti** - street grime.

**Bowling alley** - a place where pin pals meet.

**Dogma** - a puppy's mother.

**Ventriloquist** - a person who enjoys talking to himself.

**Bee** - a real buzz word.

**Wind** - air that's late for school.

**Astronomer** - a night watchman.

**Theory** - a college-educated guess.

**Cloud bank** - a place to save money for a rainy day.

**Pastry chef** - a bake-up artist.

**Fitness trainer** - a person who lives off the fat of the land.

**Hair colorist** - a dyeing breed.

**Snowball fight** - an old-fashioned cold war.

**Pioneer** - an early American who was lucky enough to find his way out of the forest.

**Meteorite** - a space chip.

**Credit card** - a debt charger.

**Tears** - remorse code.

**Time-out chair** - a sit calm.

**Ski jump** - a soar spot.

**Proofreader** - a book marker.

**Dilate** - to live a long, long time.

**Counterfeit money** - pseudough.

**Coincide** - what you should do if it rains.

**Krakatoa** - what can happen if you walk into a wall.

**Sleeping bag** - a nap sack.

**Windbag** - a person who is hard of listening.

**Claustrophobia** - a fear of Santa.

**Bandage** - the average age of a music group.

**Ignite** - an eskimo's bedtime.

**Batman** - the secret identity of Dracula.

**Magician** - anyone who can score 100% on a math test.

**Fax** - the truth

**Engineers** - ears on an engine.

**Satire** - sitting in a tall chair.

**Yoga** - a cartoon bear.

**Feedback** - when someone gets sick.

**Rosette** - a tiny rose.

**Scholastic** - what holds up your shorts.

**Vest** - opposite of East.

**Unleaded** - empty pencil case.

**Shamrock** - a plant pretending to be a stone.

**Electrocute** - a pretty electrician.

**Flash bulb** - a light bulb that thinks highly of itself.

**Racquet** - noise made by tennis player.

**Capacity** - the size of your head.

**Germinate** - bacteria in bad food.

**Jargon** - a stolen jar.

**Logarithm** - music played with pieces of wood.

**Orchid** - a baby orchestra.

**Salad dressing** - what salad does in the morning.

**Coconut** - someone who really loves cocoa.

**Caterpillar** - a column used to hold up a cat's home.

**Gruesome** - the wrong way to tell some one they have gotten taller.

**Vegetable** - where vegetarians eat their meals.

**Beverage** - slightly better than average.

**Viper** - a snake used to clean a car windshield.

**Waiter** - the first thing a monster eats in a restaurant.

**Yankee doodle** - an American drawing.

**Zombie** - an undead bee.

**Cheesecake** - served at a mouse's birthday party.

**Bacon** - what you eat on fry day.

**Greenhouse** - a home for aliens.

**Puffin** - a breathless bird.

**Reptile** - a flat lizard that hangs out on your bathroom floor.

**Canary** - a bird that comes in a tin.

**Kitten** - when a cat tells you a joke.

**Ideogram** - a telegram sent by an idiot.

**Monkey** - what an ape uses to open a door.

**Gorilla** - what a chimp uses to cook food.

**Raining cats and dogs** - don't step in the poodle.

**Eel** - fish with a cold.

**Mexican** - a can full of Mexies.

**Rose petal** - what you have on a rose bicycle.

**Slippers** -shoes made from banana skins.

**Polygon** - an escaped parrot.

**Water polo** - a sport you need a sea horse for.

**Sandwich** - a witch at the beach.

**Megahertz** - what you feel when a computer falls on your foot.

**Macintosh** - waterproof computer

# Waiter, Waiter

Waiter, Waiter there's a bee
in my soup!
**Of course, it's alphabet soup.**

Waiter, how hot are your
tamales?
**Well, if more than three
customers eat them at the same
time the sprinkler system
goes off.**

What cereal do cool rappers eat?
**Cheeri-Yo-Yo-Yo!**

Waiter, what's this insect
in my soup?
**How should I know. I'm a wait-
er, not an entomologist.**

Waiter, this apple pie
tastes like glue!
**Oh that must be peach pie. Our
apple pie tastes like plaster.**

A swap meet
**I'll trade you my hot dog for
your hamburger.**

Waiter, there's a footprint
on my lunch!
**I know sir, you told me to step
on it.**

Waiter, where should we sit to
be served quickly?
**How about at the restaurant
next door.**

Diner: How's the chicken
soup today?
**Waiter: A little fowl.**

Waiter, I can't find one clam in my clam chowder!

**Oh, and I suppose you expect to find angels in your angel food cake?**

Waiter, there's a fly in my soup.

**No sir, that's just dirt in the shape of a fly.**

Waiter, there are two flies
in my soup!
**That's ok sir, the extra one
is at no charge.**

Waiter, there's a fly in my soup!
**Don't worry sir, the frog should
surface any minute.**

Waiter, I don't see any chocolate
cake on the menu.
**No, I wiped it off.**

Waiter, do you have frog legs?
**Yes sir, this is a busy restaurant and they keep us hopping.**

Waiter, there's a fly in my soup!
**Shhh! You'll have to be quiet or everyone will want one.**

Waiter, your thumb is in my soup!
**That's ok, it's not hot.**

Waiter, you aren't fit
to serve a pig!
**I'm doing my best, sir!**

Waiter, there's a mosquito
in my soup!
**I'm sorry sir. We've run
out of flies.**

Waiter, there's a fly in my soup!
**I'm sorry sir, I'm a waiter,
not a lifeguard.**

Waiter, I can't eat this!
Why not sir?
**Because you haven't given
me a knife and fork.**

Waiter, bring me a greasy
fried egg and luke-warm,
mushy potatoes.
**We don't serve that kind
of food here sir.**
You did yesterday!

Waiter, there's a small
slug in the salad.
**I'm sorry, ma'am would you
like a bigger one?**

Waiter, there's a spider drowning
in my soup!
**It hardly looks deep enough
for that sir!**

Waiter, there's a spider
on my food!
**I'm sorry, no pets allowed!**

What's worse than finding a worm in your apple?
**Finding half a worm.**

Waiter, what is this cockroach doing on my ice cream!
**Skiing Sir!**

Waiter, what is this creepy-crawly doing in my salad?
**Not him again, he's in here every night.**

Waiter, there's a frog in my soup!
**He must be looking for the fly.**

Waiter, why is your hand on my steak? Are you crazy?
**No, do you want it to fall on the floor again?**

Did you hear about the new restaurant on the moon?
**Great food, but no atmosphere.**

Waiter: How did you find
your steak?
**Diner: Accidentally. I moved
the potato and there it was.**


How many fast food workers does
it take to change a lightbulb?
**Two. One to change it and one
to add fries with it.**

How many cafeteria ladies does it take to change a lightbulb? **None. It's better not to see the food.**

A guy ordered pizza, and Luigi asked him if he wanted his pizza in four slices or eight. "Better make it four slices, 'cause I can't eat eight."

**Waiter, I'll have a slice
of pie, please.**

Would you like anything
with that, Sir?

**Well, if it's anything like last
time, I'd better have a
hammer and chisel.**

Why do waiters prefer
elephants to flies?

**Have you ever heard of anyone
complaining about an elephant
in their soup?**

**Waiter: Would you like dinner, sir?**
Diner: Yes, what are the choices?
**Waiter: Yes and No.**

What was the reporter doing at the ice cream shop?
**Getting the scoop.**

Waiter, will the pancakes be long?
**No, round.**

Waiter, there's a fly in my soup. **Yes sir, it's the rotting meat that attracts them!**

Waiter, there's no chicken in this chicken soup! **Good, there's no horse in the horseradish either.**

How many waiter's does it take to change a lightbulb? **Three. Two to stand around complaining about it and one to get the manager.**

A customer continually complained to the waiter about the restaurant being too cold. Then he complained that it was too hot. The waiter was very patient. Finally, a second customer asked the waiter why he didn't throw out the pest. "Oh, I don't care," said the waiter with a smile. "We don't even have an air conditioner."

Waiter, there's a fly in my soup!
**Don't worry sir, that spider on your bread will get him.**

Waiter, I'd like a steak please, and make it lean.
**Forward or backward?**

Waiter, what is this stuff? That's bean salad.
**I know what it's been, but what is it now?**

Diner: Why have you given me my food in a feedbag?
**Waiter: The head waiter says you eat like a horse.**

Waiter, is this steak or chicken?
**Can't you tell?**
No, I can't
**Then why does it matter!**

Waiter, there's a fly in my soup.
**Couldn't be, sir. The cook used them in the raisin bread.**

Waiter, where is my order
of escargot?
**I'm sorry sir, you know how
snails are.**

Waiter, there's a cockroach
on my steak!
**They don't seem to care what
they eat, do they?**

Waiter, this plate is wet.
**That's your soup sir!**

Waiter: Hey! What about my tip?
**Diner: Oh yes...I forgot. Don't
ever eat here.**

What do you call a frozen
frankfurter?
**A chili dog.**

Waiter, there's a button
in my soup!
**Oh thank goodness, I've been
looking everywhere for that.**

# Diner Lingo

**Axle grease**: butter

**Baled hay**: shredded wheat.

**Birdseed**: cereal.

**Black cow**: chocolate milkshake.

**Bubble dancer**: dishwasher.

**Moo Juice**: milk.

**Bossy in a bowl**: beef stew.

**Bowl of red**: chili.

**Bucket of cold mud**: a bowl of chocolate ice cream.

**Bun pup or Bow Wow**: a hot dog.

**Burn one:** put a hamburger on the grill.

**Burn the British:** a toasted English muffin.

**C.J. Boston:** cream cheese and jelly.

**Chopper:** a table knife.

**City juice:** water.

**Cowboy:** a western omelet.

**Cow feed**: a salad.

**Dough well done with a cow to cover:** buttered toast.

**Dog biscuit:** crackers.

**Fifty-five:** a glass of root beer.

**Fly cake**: raisin bread.

**Go for a walk or On wheels:** a take out order.

**Flop two:** two eggs over easy.

**Fry two, let the sun shine:** two fried eggs with unbroken yokes.

**gravel train:** sugar bowl.

**Hemorrhage:** ketchup.

**Hold the hail:** a drink with no ice.

**Hot Top:** hot chocolate.

**High and dry:** a plain sandwich with nothing on it.

**Houseboat:** a banana split.

**In the alley:** served as a side dish.

**Keep off the grass:** no lettuce.

**Lighthouse:** a bottle of ketchup.

**Lumber:** toothpick.

**On the hoof:** meat cooked rare.

**Paint it red:** put ketchup on it.

**Mike and Ike:** salt and pepper.

**Mississippi Mud or Yellow Paint:** mustard.

**Nervous pudding:** gelatin.

**Put a hat on it:** add ice cream.

**Raft**: toast.

**Sand**: sugar.

**Sea dust:** salt

**Shake one in the hay:** strawberry milkshake.

**Shingle with a shimmy and shake:** buttered toast with jam or jelly.

**Sinkers and suds:** doughnut and coffee.

**Soup jockey**: waitress.

**Spot with a twist**: tea with lemon.

**Squeeze one:** a glass of orange juice.

**Throw it in the mud:** add chocolate syrup.

**Warts:** olives.

**Wax:** American cheese.

**White cow:** vanilla milkshake.

**Wreck'ém:** scramble the eggs.

# Eat Your Words

Do not underestimate the power of the chocolate side of the force!

Red meat isn't bad for you. Fuzzy, green meat is bad for you!

Everybody needs something to believe in. I believe I'll have another slice of pizza.

Evolution created anchovies. Human stupidity put them on pizza.

# Food Advice:

-Never trust a dog to watch your food.
-Don't sneeze when you're eating crackers.
-You can't hide broccoli in a glass of milk.
-School lunches stick to the wall.
-Don't ever be too full for dessert.
-Beware of a school lunch that is moving.
-Never ask your little brother to hold a tomato.

Indigestion is what you get when a square meal doesn't fit in a round tummy.

Did you hear about the cannibal who loved fast food? **He ordered a pizza with everybody on it.**

# School Daze

Principal: Why haven't you been in school?

**Student: It's not my fault. I can't cross the road in front of the school.**

Principal: Why not:

**Student: Because there is a guy standing there with a sign that says "Stop Children Crossing"!**

The school lunches are full of iron, which is probably why they are so difficult to chew.

Math Teacher: If you multiply 1345 by 678, what would you get?
**Student: The wrong answer!**

Why did the boy throw his watch out the window during the history test?
**He wanted to see time fly.**

What's the difference between your school and your principal's car?
**One breaks up and the other breaks down.**

Why are teachers like doctors?
**Because they are both good at giving exams.**

Where do martians train to be teachers?
**Mooniversity.**

How many teachers does it take to work the photocopier?
**Who cares, as long as they are out of the classroom.**

Teacher: Is your father helping you with your homework?
**Student: No, he knows less than I do on this.**

What did the teacher say when he lost his pencil?
**"Where's my pencil."**

What do math teachers use to unclog their sinks?
**They work it out with a pencil.**

What is an English teacher's
favorite fruit?
**The Grapes of Wrath.**

Did you hear about the cross-eyed
teacher who had to retire?
**He couldn't control his pupils.**

Teacher: How many letters are
there in the alphabet?
**Student: 11!**
Teacher: Why did you guess that?
**Student: t-h-e-a-l-p-h-a-b-e-t**

Why do robot teachers
never get scared?
**They have nerves of steel.**

Teacher: How can you tell the age of a
tree monkey?
**Student: Cut it in half and
count the rings?**

Why did the teacher chose that kid
to be her teacher's pet?
**Because he looks the most
like her dog.**

Why was the teacher chased by a hen?
**Because he said he was being paid chicken feed.**

Teacher: If we do the 10 times table, 10 times, how many times will we have done it?
**Student: "Is this a trick question?"**

Why are you taking a sponge to class?
**I want to absorb everything.**

Where do crazy teachers go to school?
**Loony-versity.**

Did you hear about the science teacher who played tricks on people?
**He is a real particle joker.**

Math teacher: Today we are going to find the lowest common denominator.
**Student: Geez, haven't they found that yet. My Dad says they were looking for that when he was a kid.**

Did you hear about the geography teacher who mapped out her career?

Or the archaeology teacher whose job was in ruins?

Did you hear about the P.E. teacher who used to run around the classroom trying to jog kids' memories?

What's the difference between a train and a teacher?
**A train says "choo-choo", but a teacher says "get that gum out of your mouth this instant."**

What's the best snake to take to math class?
**An adder.**

What is the best way to tell your math teacher that you forgot your homework–again!
**Long distance!**

What is the easiest way to get a day off of school?
**Wait until Saturday.**

A bottle of soda went to school, what subject was it going to learn?
**Fizzical Education.**

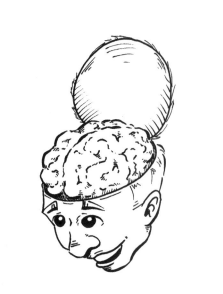

Student: YUK! This lunch tastes like soap!
**Cafeteria Lady: At least you know the kitchen is clean.**

What is the best part of school?
**Summer vacation.**

Principal: Why are you always late for school?
**Student: It's not my fault, you always ring the bell before I get here!**

# Silly School Excuses

My agent won't allow me to publish my homework until the movie deal is finalized.

My grandmother sat on my laptop.

Can you define "homework"?

I plead the 5th.

Our furnace stopped working and we had to burn it so we wouldn't freeze.

Here it is. I wrote it in invisible ink.

My dog ate it, and then my science
project ate my dog.

It was so perfect, I'm having it framed.

I forgot to remember.

I dropped it in the street and
a car parked on it.

I was afraid I'd lose it, so
I mailed it to you.

I dreamed I did it and turned it in.

It ran away.

I had an excuse, but I forgot it.

There wasn't any toilet paper in
the bathrooms here at school, so
I used my homework.

You're the best teacher in the world, and I love your shirt, oh and I love the way you've done your hair...I haven't done my homework...but an A for effort would be nice.

I was working on my homework and watching the news, when they said that the paper I was using had been recalled due to explosive fibers. So, I took it back to the store and they guaranteed I would have some paper in 3-5 weeks.

I was standing in the Principal's office when I accidentally dropped it into the paper shredder.

I got my homework done early and left it in the living room. When I came back into the room, it had spontaneously combusted.

I got food poisoning from the school lunch, and was physically unable to do my homework.

The science teacher didn't have any paper, so I donated my homework so he could demonstate the effects of hydro-chloric acid on paper.

I was doing my homework last night. I got up to get a drink from the fridge. When I came back, my homework was gone, but I saw little green footprints leading under the bed.

My babysitter flushed my homework down the toilet.

A Teacher's excuse - I am sorry your exams are not all graded. The cat got jealous as I was marking instead of paying attention to him. After I went to bed, he attacked the test papers.

My locker jammed and I couldn't get my homework out.

I was late for school because all the clocks in the house stopped at the same time.

I'm leading a protest to protect the trees.

I was finishing it on the way to school this morning, but a big wind blew it out the window.

I couldn't do my homework because it was dark outside.

There weren't any commercials during the TV show I was watching.

I woke up this morning and couldn't remember anything. Who are you? Where am I? Who am I? What homework?

Homework? I was supposed to bring it back to school? I thought it was suppose to stay home.

My brother grabbed my homework by mistake.

Didn't you feel the earthquake?

A mouse bit a hole in the bottom of my backpack and ate the edge of my homework.

When I saw the homework assignment, it scared me so much that it put me into shock for the next 18 hours.

I'm translating it from Klingon.

I'm sorry I was late, but it was because there are eight kids in my family, and my mother set the alarm for seven.

My parents couldn't finish it, so they took it to work to get some help.

My younger brother finished my homework and turned it into his teacher to show how smart he is.

The Press Secretary called and asked me to rework the president's speech on economic affairs. Do I get extra credit?

I left it in my shirt and my mother thought it was a dryer sheet.

Too much knowledge is a dangerous thing, and I don't want to hurt myself.

I was kidnapped by aliens who kept it for further study. They gave me an "A".

And FBI agent came by last night. He picked up my homework, memorized it, then ate it.

My son is under a doctor's care and
should not take P.E. today.
Please execute him.

The Boy Scouts were showing us
how to build a fire and they
used my homework.

I gave it to charity. There are
kids who are less fortunate than me.

I used it as scratch paper for
my homework excuses list.

Everything I ever needed to know,
I learned in kindergarten.

The Smithsonian Institution
requested it for an exhibit.

I didn't do it, because I didn't want to add
to your already heavy workload.

# Hysterical History

Who succeeded the first
President of the United States?
**The second one.**

How did people react when
electricity was invented?
**They were shocked!**

Why does history keep
repeating itself?
**Because we didn't learn
it the first time.**

When was Rome built?
**At night.**
Why do you say that?
**Because Rome wasn't
built in a day.**

What did Caesar say
to Cleopatra?
**Toga-ether we can
rule the world.**

Why did Julius Caesar
buy crayons?
**He wanted to
Mark Antony.**

Why did the Romans
build straight roads?
**Because chariots didn't
come with steering wheels.**


How would you discover what life
was like in Ancient Egypt?
**Ask your mummy!**


How did Vikings
send messages?
**By Norse code.**

Where did the Pilgrims land?
**On their feet!**


Who invented fractions?
**Henry the 1/8th**


Whose son was Edward, the black prince?
**Old King Cole.**


Who invented Arthur's round table?
**Sir Cumference.**

Why was the ghost of Anne Bolynn always chasing King Henry?
**She was trying to get ahead.**

Where was the Magna Carta signed?
**On the bottom.**

What was Camelot?
**A place where people parked their camels.**

Why did Robin Hood steal
from the rich?
**The poor didn't have
anything to steal.**

What did the Sheriff of Nottingham
say when Robin Hood shot
an arrow at him?
**That was an arrow escape.**

My teacher reminds me of history.
**She's always repeating herself.**

**Student: I wish I was born 1000 years ago!**

Teacher: Why?

**Student: Because then I wouldn't have to learn so much history.**


Let's learn about Ancient History. **We'll talk over old times.**


If Spanish explorers went around the world in a galleon, I wonder how many miles they got to the galleon.

What was the first thing that Queen Elizabeth did as she ascended the throne?
**Sat down.**

Who was the biggest thief in history?
**Atlas, he held up the whole world.**

What was Camelot famous for?
**It's knight life.**

When were King Arthur's armies too tired to fight? **When they had a lot of sleepless knights.**

What did Napoleon become on his 41st birthday? **A year older.**

How did Columbus' men sleep on the Santa Maria? **With their eyes closed.**

What is a forum?
**Two-um plus two-um.**

Why was George Washington
buried at Mount Vernon?
**Because he was dead.**

Mom: Why aren't you doing
well in history?
**Kid: Because the teacher keeps
talking about things that
happened before I was born.**

Where is Hadrian's Wall?
**Around Hadrian's Garden.**

Why was early history called
the Dark Ages?
**Because there were
so many knights.**

Why did Arthur have
a round table?
**So no one could corner him.**

What kind of bus crossed
the Atlantic?
**ColumBUS.**

Do you know the 20th President
of the United States?
**No, we were never introduced.**

Where did knights learn
to kill dragons?
**At knight school.**

What did Paul Revere say
to his horse?
**Giddy-up.**

When a knight died in battle, what
did they put on his gravestone?
**Rust in Peace**

What did they do at the
Boston Tea Party?
**I don't know, I wasn't invited.**

Why did the pioneers cross the
Great Plains in covered wagons?
**They didn't want to wait
40 years for a train.**

How did you do on your
final exams?
**Like George Washington.
I went down in history.**

Abraham Lincoln had to walk seven miles to and from school everyday. **Why didn't he take the bus like everyone else?**

Why did George Washington stand up in the boat that crossed the Delaware? **He was afraid if he sat down, someone would give him an oar to row.**

Where was the Declaration of Independence signed? **On the bottom.**

What did Paul Revere say at the end of his midnight ride?
**Whoa!**

What do you get if you cross a canyon with a Revolutionary War hero?
**Gorge Washington.**

What did Paul Revere Octopus yell?
**Two arms! Four arms! Six arms! Eight arms!**

Where did King Tut go
to ease his back pain?
**To a Cairo-practor.**

Why did Ancient Romans
close down the Coliseum?
**Because the lions were
eating all the prophets.**

Why did Cleopatra take milk baths?
**She couldn't find a cow
tall enough for a milk shower.**

Why is it so wet in England?
**Because kings and queens
have always reigned there.**

Why were the pilgrim's pants
always falling down?
**Because they wore their belts
around their hats.**

Why didn't the dinosaur skeleton
just walk out of the museum?
**It didn't have the guts.**

# Brain Teasers
# Riddle me this!

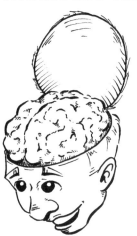

You throw away the
outside and cook the
inside. Then you eat the
outside and throw away
the inside.
What did you eat?

What gets wetter and wetter the more it dries?

A Towel.

What can you catch but not throw?

A cold.

I have holes in my top and bottom, my left and right, and in the middle. But I still hold water. What am I?

A sponge.

I run around all day.
Under the bed at night
I'm not alone. My tongue
hangs up and out,
I'm filled in the morning.
What am I?

A shoe.

I can run but not walk.
Wherever I go, thought
follows close behind.
What am I?

Your nose.

How many coins
can you put in
an empty jar?

One. After that it isn't empty.

What goes around the
world but stays in a
corner?

A stamp.

Give me food, and I live;
give me water,
and I die.
What am I?

Fire.

What can run but never walks, has a mouth but never talks, has a head but never weeps, has a bed but never sleeps?

A river.

No sooner spoken than broken. What is it?

A secret.

Step on me, and I won't break. But in the ocean, I will. What am I?

A wave.

I never was, am
yet to be,
No one ever saw me,
nor ever will,
And yet, I am the
hope of all
To live and breathe
on earth.
What am I?

Tomorrow

Pronounced as one letter,
And written with three,
Two letters there are,
And two only in me.
I'm double, I'm single,
I'm black, blue, and gray,
I'm read from both ends,
And the same either way.
What am I?

An eye.

The man who invented it doesn't want it. The man who bought it doesn't need it. The man who needs it doesn't know it. What is it?

A coffin.

I am weightless, but you can see me. Put me in a bucket, and I'll make it lighter. What am I?

A hole.

From the beginning
of eternity
To the end of time
and space
To the beginning of
every end
And the end of
every place.
What am I?

Where does yesterday
follow today, and
tomorrow's in the middle?

A Dictionary.

I'm light as a feather, yet
the strongest man can't
hold me for much more
than a minute.
What am I?

Breath

I'm the part of the bird that's not in the sky. I can swim in the ocean and yet remain dry.
What am I?

A shadow.

In a marble hall white as milk
Lined with skin as soft as silk
Within a fountain crystal-clear
A golden apple doth appear.
No doors there are to this
stronghold,
Yet thieves break in to steal its
gold.
–Mother Goose

An egg.

I went into the woods and got it. I sat down to seek it. I brought it home with me because I couldn't find it. What am I?

A splinter.

At night they come
without being fetched,
and by day they are lost
without being stolen.
What are they?

The stars.

All about, but cannot
be seen,
Can be captured, cannot
be held,
No voice, but can
be heard.
What is it?

The wind.

If you break me,
I do not stop working.
If you touch me,
I may be snared.
If you lose me,
Nothing will matter.
What am I?

Your heart.

If a man carried my
burden,
He would break his back.
I am not rich,
But I leave silver in my
track.
What am I?

Glittering points that
downward thrust,
Sparkling spears that
never rust.
What is it?

An icicle.

Weight in my belly,
Trees on my back,
Nails in my ribs,
Feet I lack.
What am I?

A ship.

Until I am measured,
I am not known.
Yet how you miss me,
When I have flown!
What am I?

Time.

My life can be
measured in hours;
I serve by being devoured.
Thin, I am quick; fat,
I am slow.
Wind is my foe.
What am I?

A candle.

Lighter than what I'm
made of,
More of me is hidden than
is seen.
What am I?

An Iceberg.

One is sitting and will never get up. The second eats as much as is given to him, yet is always hungry. The third goes away and never returns. What are they?

A fireplace, fire, and smoke.

When I am filled,
I can point the way;
When I am empty,
Nothing moves me.
I have two skins,
One without and one
within.
What am I?

I fly, yet I have no wings.
I cry, yet I
have no eyes.
Darkness
follows me;
lower light I
never see.

A cloud.

What walks on four legs in the morning, two at mid-day, and three in the evening?

A human. As a baby, it crawls; in old age, uses a cane.

What is it that, after you take away the whole, some still remains?

The word "wholesome."

What is made of wood, but cannot be sawed?

Sawdust.

I have hands that wave at
you,
Though I never say
goodbye.
It's cool for you to be with
me.
What am I?

An electric fan

# Belly Laughs
## (The doctor will see you now!)

Doctor, I can't get to sleep
at night!
**Sleep on a windowsill,
you'll soon drop off.**


Doctor, I haven't stopped
laughing since my operation!
**I told you I'd have you
in stitches.**

Doctor, are you sure my
arteries are clogged?
**I'm the doctor,
I aorta know.**

Doctor, I keep imagining that
I'm on a sunken ship and I'm
really worried.
**It looks like you're a
nervous wreck.**

Doctor, I feel as sick as a dog!
**Then, make an appointment
with the vet.**


Doctor, I got trampled by a
bunch of cows.
**I herd that!**

Doctor, I think I have
a split personality!
**Then, you'll have
to pay twice.**


Doctor, I think I'm
an alligator!
**Don't worry, you'll
snap out of it.**

**Doctor, is there really a pill
to improve memory?**
Yes, how many would
you like?
**How many would I
like of what?**

Why did the angry doctor
have to retire?
**Because he lost his patients.**

**Doctor, I swallowed a chicken bone!**
Are you choking?
**No, I'm serious.**

Doctor, I have a button stuck up my nose, what should I do?
**Breathe through the four little holes.**

Why do surgeons wear masks?
**So no one knows who they are if they make a mistake.**

**Doctor, doctor, I've been stung by a wasp!**
Did you put anything on it?
**No, the wasp seemed to enjoy it.**

Did you hear about the foot doctor who ran for mayor? **He was defeated.**

Doctor, my job at the Laundromat is wearing me out. **You do look a little washed out.**

**Psychiatrist: I see you're reading the telephone book.** Are you enjoying it? **The plot is terrible, but what a cast of characters!**

Nurse, can you take this patient's temperature?
**Sure doctor, where should I take it?**

Doctor, I feel like $20.
**Go shopping. The change will do you good.**

Show me a kid with braces on his teeth...and I'll show you a parent who puts his money where his kid's mouth is.

What do you call an eye doctor who lives on an island in the Bering Sea?
**An optical Aleutian.**

Psychiatrist: Do you find you have trouble making decisions?
**Patient: Well, yes and no.**

Why does the dentist always seem sad?
**Because he's so down in the mouth.**

**Student: I better send this math test to a doctor.**

Teacher: why?

**Student: I just can't figure out the problems.**

My doctor's always changes her mind. First she says she'll treat me, and then she makes me pay.

**Research scientist: I've found the cure!**
Assistant: For what disease?
**Research scientist: I haven't found that yet!**

Doctor: I wouldn't worry about talking to yourself.
**Patient: But Doc, I'm such a bore!**

Doctor, can you help me?
My teenage son thinks he's a
refrigerator.
**Don't worry. He'll chill out.**

**Doctor, can you get the
quarter out of my ear?**
Goodness! Why didn't you
come to me sooner?
**I didn't need the money
until now.**

# How are you feeling?

"I should have my head examined,"
Said Mr. Cabbage.

"I need my eyes checked," said Mr.
Potato.

"I feel run down," said Mrs. Beet.

"I hurt in the pit of my stomach," said
Ms. Plum.

"I have hay fever," said Mr. Bale.

Doctor, is there a cure for flat feet?
**Yes, a foot pump.**

Doctor, what should I do if my ear rings?
**Answer it!**

Doctor, I have a fish stuck in my ear!

**I'm sending you to a specialist. You have a serious herring problem.**

Doctor, should I surf the Internet on an empty stomach?

**No, you should do it on a computer.**

Doctor, I have gas! What
should I do?
**Go fill up my car!**

Doctor, I feel like a sheep.
**That's baaaaaad!**

Nurse: How is the girl who swallowed the quarter?

**Doctor: No change yet.**

School Nurse: Have you ever had problems with appendicitis?

**Student: Only when I try to spell it.**

What did the X-ray of my head show?
**Nothing.**

Doctor, I think I'm a calculator.
**Then you should have no problem taking your math test.**

Doctor, you have to help me out!
**Which way did you come in?**

Doctor, everyone thinks
I'm a liar.
**That's hard to believe.**

Doctor, I think there are
two of me!
**One at a time, please.**

Doctor, I swallowed
my harmonica.
**Good thing you don't
play the piano.**

Doctor, I feel like an apple. **We must get to the core of the problem.**

Doctor, I snore so loud, I keep myself awake. **Well, then sleep in another room.**

Doctor, I'm having trouble breathing!
**Don't worry. I'll put a stop to that.**


Doctor, everyone keeps ignoring me.
**Next, please.**

Doctor, I'm becoming invisible.
**I can see you're not all there.**

Doctor, I think I need glasses.
**You certainly do. This is a restaurant.**

I feel like a deck of cards!
**We'll deal with that later.**

Doctor, I think I'm
a caterpillar.
**Don't worry. You'll
change soon.**

Doctor, I think I'm a yo-yo.
**Oh? Feeling up and down?**

Doctor, I broke my arm
in two places.
**Well, don't go back to those
places again.**

**Doctor: I have some bad news and some worse news.**

Patient: Give me the bad news.

**Doctor: Your lab tests came back and you have 24 hours to live.**

Patient: What could be worse than that?

**Doctor: I've been trying to reach you since yesterday.**

**Doctor, I feel like a frog.**
What does that mean?
**That I'm going to croak.**

A man walks into a doctor's office. He has a cucumber up his nose, a carrot in his left ear and a banana in his right ear. "What's the matter with me?" he asks the doctor. The doctor replies, "You're not eating properly."

What's the difference between a general doctor and a specialist?

**One treats what you have, the other thinks you have what he treats.**

At the doctor's office, a woman touched her right knee with her index finger and yelled, "Ow, that hurts." Then she touched her left cheek, and again yelled, "Ouch! That hurts, too." Then she touched her right earlobe, "Ow, even THAT hurts", she cried. The doctor checked her for a moment and said, "You have a broken finger."

# Chicken Jokes

**Why did the chicken cross the road?**
To prove to the possum it could actually be done!

**A farmer with a lot of chickens posted this sign:**
Free chickens. Our coop runneth over.

**Why did the chicken cross the road twice?**
Because it was a double-crosser.

A man was driving along a freeway when he noticed a chicken running alongside the car. He was amazed to see the chicken keeping up with him, because he was doing 50 mph (80 km/h). He accelerated to 60 mph (97 km/h), and the chicken stayed right next to him. Then, the chicken passed him. The man noticed that the chicken had three legs. So he followed the chicken to the farm down the road, and he asked the farmer, "What's up with your chickens?" The farmer said "Well, everybody likes chicken legs, so I bred a three-legged bird. I'm going to be a millionaire." The man asked him how they tasted. The farmer said, "Don't know, haven't caught one yet."

**Why did the Turkey cross the road?**
To prove he wasn't a chicken.

**Why did the dinosaur cross the road?**
Because chickens hadn't evolved yet.

**Why did the horse cross the road?**
Because the chicken needed a day off.

**Why did the squirrel cross the road?**
Because he was taped to the chicken.

**Why did the chicken cross the playground?**
To get to the other slide.

**Why did the cow cross the road?**
To get to the udder side.

**Why did the turtle cross the road?**
To get to the shell station.

**Why did the chicken cross the basketball court?**
He heard the referee call fowl.

**What do you call a frightened scuba diver?**
Chicken of the sea.

**What do you get when you cross a chicken with a guitar?**
A chicken that makes music when you pluck it.

**What do you get when you cross a chicken with a bell?**
An alarm cluck.

**What do you get when you cross a chicken with a dog?**
A hen that lays pooched eggs.

**What is a haunted chicken?**
A poultry-geist.

**Is it okay to eat fried chicken with your fingers?**
No, the fingers should be eaten separately.

**What is the difference between a chicken and an elephant?**

An elephant can get chicken pox, but a chicken can't get elephant pox.

**What kind of tree does a chicken come from?**

A Poul-tree.

**Why don't chickens like people?**

They beat eggs.

**Why did the rooster run away?**
He was a chicken.

**Why did the chicken cross the Internet?**
To get to the other site.

**Which day of the week do chickens hate most?**
Fry-day!

**Is chicken soup good for your health?**
Not if you're a chicken.

**What did one chicken say to the other after walking through poison ivy?**
You scratch my beak and I'll scratch yours.

**What is Superchicken's real identity?**
Cluck Kent

**What happened when the hen ate cement?**

She laid a sidewalk.

**What do you get when a chicken lays an egg on top of a barn?**

An eggroll.

**What do chickens eat at birthday parties?**

Coop-cakes.

**What do chicken families do on Saturday afternoon?**
Go on pecknics.

**Why did the rooster stay outside during the hurricane?**
It was fowl weather.

**What happened to the chicken whose feathers pointed the wrong way?**
She was tickled to death.

**Why did the chicken cross the road?**
She wanted to see a man lay a brick.

**What did the man cross the road?**
He wanted to eat the chicken.

**What time do chickens go to lunch?**
Twelve o'cluck

**How do chickens dance?**
Chick to chick.

**Why did the chicken cross the state line?**
To get out of Kentucky.

**How do you know when a chicken is under arrest?**
She's wearing hencuffs.

**How long do chickens work?**
Around the cluck.

**Why were the hens lying on their backs with their legs in the air?**
Because eggs were going up.

**Which dance will a chicken not do?**
The foxtrot.

**What do you call a joke book for chickens?**
A yolk book.

**Why does a rooster watch TV?**
For hentertainment.

**How do you stop a rooster from crowing on Sunday?**
Eat him on Saturday.

**What did the chicken do when he saw the bucket of fried chicken?**
He kicked the bucket.

**On which side does a chicken have the most feathers?**
On the outside.

**What do you call a witch that likes the beach, but is scared of the water.**
A chicken sand-witch.

**What happend to the little chicken that misbehaved at school?**
It was eggspelled.

A guy wanted to start a chicken farm, so he bought a hundred chickens to start. A month later he went back and bought another hundred, saying the first hundred had died. A month later he came back again to buy another hundred, because the second batch had died too. He tells the chicken farmer, "I think I know what I'm doing wrong. I'm planting them too deep."

**Why should a school not be near a chicken farm?**

So the pupils don't overhear fowl language.

**What do you call a team of chickens playing football?**

Fowl play

**What do you get when you cross a chicken with gum?**

Chicklets.

**Why do chickens lay eggs?**
Because they become egg-cited.

**What do you call the chicken that crossed the road?**
Poultry in motion.

**Why did the possum cross the road?**
It didn't.

**Why did the chicken cross the road?**
Because it could.

# Word Play

Oxymorons: A figure of speech composed of two contradictory words.

# Jumbo Shrimp

# Same Difference

# Pretty Ugly

# Definite Maybe

Virtual Reality

Only Choice

Alone Together

Larger Half

Extinct Life

Seriously Funny

Liquid Gas

Almost Exactly

Genuine Imitation

Freezer Burn

Rolling Stop

Working Holiday

Civil Engineer

Found Missing

Open Secret

Minor Crisis

Exact Estimate

Original Copies

Great Depression

Sweet Tart

Silent Scream

Good Grief

Near Miss

Old News

Criminal Justice

Crash Landing

Sweet Sorrow

Hot Chili

**Palindromes:** *Words or phrases that can be read the same in both directions.*

# Eye

# Racecar

# Was it Eliot's toilet I saw?

# Never odd or even.

Don't nod

Too bad - I hid a boot

No trace, not one carton

Some men interpret
nine memos

Malapropisms: *hilarious verbal slips and word goofs.*

He had to use a fire distinguisher.

Dad says the monster is a pigment of my imagination.

Good punctuation means not to be late.

"Shouldn't" is a contraption.

My father is a civil serpent.

It is beyond my apprehension.

"We cannot let terrorists and rogue nations hold this nation hostile or hold our allies hostile."
- George W. Bush

They will dissolve the mystery.

Abraham Lincoln wrote the Gettysburg Address while traveling from Washington to Gettysburg on the back of an envelope.

An oral contract isn't worth the paper it's printed on.

History is full of interesting caricatures.

Damp weather is very hard on the sciences.

The flood was so bad they had
to evaporate the city.

Flying saucers are an optical conclusion.

I sent the package by partial post.

How would you like to write
my autobiography?

The Indian squabs carried porpoises on
their back.

Tongue Twisters:   *Attempting to recite a rhyme or phrase as fast as you can without tripping over the verbal challenges.*

How much wood would a woodchuck chuck,
If a woodchuck could chuck wood?
He would chuck, he would, as much as he could,
And chuck as much as a woodchuck would.
If a woodchuck could chuck wood.

Unique New York

Many an anemone sees an enemy anemone.

# Greek Grapes

Imagine an imaginary menagerie manager imagining managing an imaginary menagerie.

Freshly-fried flying fish.

What noise annoys an oyster? The nose that annoys an oyster is a noise that knows no oyster.

A tutor who tooted the flute
tried to tutor two tooters to toot.
Said the two to their tutor:
"Is it harder to toot,
Or to tutor two tooters to toot?"

A big black bear hit a big black bug and
the big black bug bled black blood.

Theophilus Thistle, the Thistle Sifter,
Sifted a sieve of unsifted thistles.
If Theophilus Thistle, the Thistle Sifter,
Sifted a Sieve of unsifted thistles,
Where is the sieve of un-sifted
thistlesTheophilus Thistle, the
Thistle Sifter, sifted?

Which wristwatches are
Swiss wristwatches?

One smart fellow; he felt smart.
Two smart fellows; they felt smart.
Three smart fellows; they all felt smart.

Mondegreens: *Misheard words and song lyrics.*

**"There's a bathroom on the right."**
Actual: "There's a bad moon on the rise."
*-Creedence Clearwater Revival*

**"I blow bubbles when you are not here."**
Actual: "My world crumbles when you are not here."
*- Macy Gray*

**"She's got a chicken to ride."**
Actual: "She's got a ticket to ride."
*-the Beatles*

"I got no towel, I hung it up again."
Actual: "I get knocked down, but I get up again."
-*Chumbawumba*

"Sont des mots qui vont tres bien ensemble, tres bien ensemble."
Actual: Sunday monkey won't play piano song, play piano song.
-*the Beatles*

"The foulest dentures in the air."
Actual: "The foulest stench is in the air."
-*Michael Jackson*

**"Donuts make my brown eyes blue."**
Actual: "Don't it make my brown eyes blue."
-Crystal Gale

**"Hope the city voted for you."**
Actual: "Hopelessly devoted to you."
-Hopelessly Devoted to You, Grease

**"Clown Control to Mao Tse-tung"**
Actual: "Ground Control to Major Tom."
-David Bowie

**"Sweet dreams are made of cheese."**
Actual: "Sweet dreams are made of this."
- *The Eurythmics*

**"Mice aroma"**
Actual: "My Sharona"
- *The Knack*

**"Gotta leave it all behind and take a cruise."**
Actual: "Gotta leave it all behind and face the truth."
- *Queen*

**"Whoa! Nipsey Russell!"**
Actual: "Roam if you want to."
-B-52's

**"The ants are my friend, they're blowin' in the wind."**
Actual: "The answer my friend, is blowin' in the wind."
-Bob Dylan

**"I'll never leave your pizza burning."**
Actual: "I'll never be your beast of burden."
-The Rolling Stones

**"Another turnip born, a fork stuck in the road."**
Actual: "Another turning point, a fork stuck in the road."
-Greenday

**"Somebody better put that bag in your face."**
Actual: "Somebody put you back in your place."
-Queen

**"What a nice surprise, when you're out of ice."**
Actual: "What a nice surprise, bring your alibis."
-Eagles

**"I've been through the desert on a horse with no legs."**
Actual: "I've been through the desert on a horse with no name."
- *America*

**"Will this stage of goo never end?"**
Actual: "Will this deja vu never end?"
- *Spice Girls*

"I had a little dove, now he's splattered on the floor."
Actual: "I had a little love, now I'm back for more."
-*Spice Girls*

"Ain't nothing but a big steak."
Actual: "Ain't nothing but a mistake"
-*Backstreet Boys*

"Dred-lock rock star."
Actual: "Rock Lobster."
-*B-52s*

**"You give love a band-aid."**
Actual: "You give love a bad name."
-Bon Jovi

**"I don't think you're ready for spaghetti."**
Actual: "I don't think you're ready for this jelly."
-Destiny's Child

**"Where the sheeps have lo mein."**
Actual: "Where the streets have no name."
-U2

**"Stepped on a Pop Tart."**
Actual: "Stepped on a pop top."
-Jimmy Buffet

"**Australians all love ostriches,
for we are young and free.**"
Actual: "Australians all, let us rejoice,
for we are young and free."
*-Australian National Anthem*

"**Oh Canada, we stand on cars and freeze.**"
Actual: "Oh Canada, we stand on guard for
thee."
*-Canadian National Anthem*

"**Jose, can you sing?**"
Actual: "Oh, say can you see?"
*-American National Anthem*

# A sense of humor is the sixth sense.

Laughter is the best medicine!